The good life
TITUS
by Tim Chester

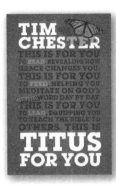

Titus For You

If you are reading *Titus For You* (see page 60) alongside this Good Book Guide, here is how the studies in this booklet link to the chapters of *Titus For You*:

Study One → Ch 1-2 Study Four → Ch 5
Study Two → Ch 3 Study Five → Ch 6-7
Study Three → Ch 4

The good life
The good book guide to Titus
© The Good Book Company/Tim Chester, 2014.
Series Consultants: Tim Chester, Tim Thornborough,
    Anne Woodcock, Carl Laferton

The Good Book Company
Tel: (US): 866 244 2165
Tel (UK): 0333 123 0880
Tel (int): + (44) 208 942 0880
Email: info@thegoodbook.co.uk

Websites
North America: www.thegoodbook.com
UK: www.thegoodbook.co.uk
Australia: www.thegoodbook.com.au
New Zealand: www.thegoodbook.co.nz

ISBN: 9781909919631

Printed in the USA

CONTENTS

introduction: good book guides

Every Bible-study group is different—yours may take place in a church building, in a home or in a cafe, on a train, over a leisurely mid-morning coffee or squashed into a 30-minute lunch break. Your group may include new Christians, mature Christians, non-Christians, moms and tots, students, businessmen or teens. That's why we've designed these *Good Book Guides* to be flexible for use in many different situations.

Our aim in each session is to uncover the meaning of a passage, and see how it fits into the "big picture" of the Bible. But that can never be the end. We also need to appropriately apply what we have discovered to our lives. Let's take a look at what is included:

⊕ **Talkabout:** Most groups need to "break the ice" at the beginning of a session, and here's the question that will do that. It's designed to get people talking around a subject that will be covered in the course of the Bible study.

⊕ **Investigate:** The Bible text for each session is broken up into manageable chunks, with questions that aim to help you understand what the passage is about. **The Leader's Guide** contains **guidance on questions**, and sometimes ☑ additional "follow-up" questions.

⊞ **Explore more (optional):** These questions will help you connect what you have learned to other parts of the Bible, so you can begin to fit it all together like a jig-saw; or occasionally look at a part of the passage that's not dealt with in detail in the main study.

⊕ **Apply:** As you go through a Bible study, you'll keep coming across **apply** sections. These are questions to get the group discussing what the Bible teaching means in practice for you and your church. ⊡ **Getting personal** is an opportunity for you to think, plan and pray about the changes that you personally may need to make as a result of what you have learned.

⊕ **Pray:** We want to encourage prayer that is rooted in God's word—in line with his concerns, purposes and promises. So each session ends with an opportunity to review the truths and challenges highlighted by the Bible study, and turn them into prayers of request and thanksgiving.

The **Leader's Guide** and introduction provide historical background information, explanations of the Bible texts for each session, ideas for **optional extra** activities, and guidance on how best to help people uncover the truths of God's word.

why study Titus?

It's A Wonderful Life is recognised by the American Film Institute as one of the 100 best American films of all time. It stars James Stewart as George Bailey, a man who in his youth dreamed of travelling the world. But along the way, he's made sacrifices for other people that mean he never got to leave his small town. Now he's a weary, broken man who, through no fault of his own, is going to be declared bankrupt. So he stands on the town bridge about to commit suicide.

But then his guardian angel intervenes. The angel gives him a vision of what life would have been like if he'd never lived. He sees that his life counts, that it has made a difference. He has truly lived a good life—a wonderful life—touching the lives of many people in small but decisive ways.

In many ways, this is what Paul is doing in the letter he writes to Titus. He is giving us a vision of a life that touches people in small but decisive ways—a life that has eternal consequences. He is setting out the truly good life.

Paul knew that truth is what produces goodness, or "godliness". What is that truth? "The hope of eternal life, which God, who does not lie, promised before the beginning of time, and which now at his appointed season he has brought to light through the preaching entrusted to me by the command of God our Saviour" (1 v 2-3). The truth that creates a good life is the gospel. That is the truth that brings life and then changes life. And this good life overflows into others' lives, too. A gospel-changed life "will make the teaching about God our Saviour attractive" (2 v 10). The good life is a missional force.

Paul wanted Titus to lead this group of Christians on Crete to be church in a way that kept the gospel central for life, growth and mission. These five studies will inspire and equip you to make sure that you do the same—so that you, as individuals and as a local church, will live the godly life, the missional life… the good life.

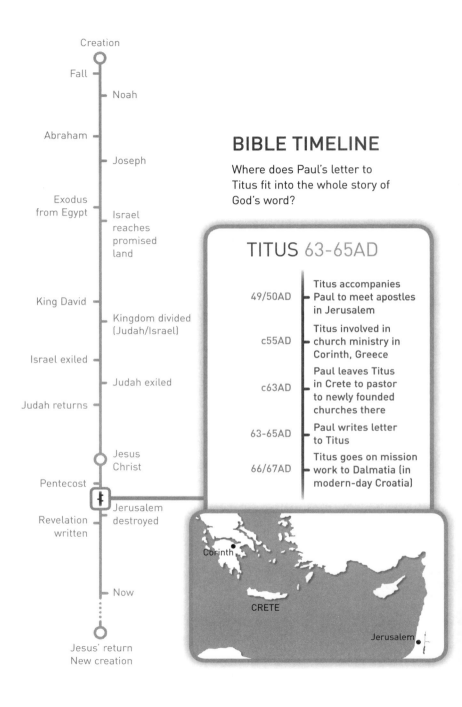

Creation

Fall

Noah

Abraham

Joseph

Exodus
from Egypt

Israel
reaches
promised
land

King David

Kingdom divided
(Judah/Israel)

Israel exiled

Judah exiled

Judah returns

Jesus
Christ

Pentecost

Jerusalem
destroyed

Revelation
written

Now

Jesus' return
New creation

BIBLE TIMELINE

Where does Paul's letter to
Titus fit into the whole story of
God's word?

TITUS 63-65AD

49/50AD	Titus accompanies Paul to meet apostles in Jerusalem
c55AD	Titus involved in church ministry in Corinth, Greece
c63AD	Paul leaves Titus in Crete to pastor to newly founded churches there
63-65AD	Paul writes letter to Titus
66/67AD	Titus goes on mission work to Dalmatia (in modern-day Croatia)

Corinth

CRETE

Jerusalem

1

Titus 1 v 1-9
LEADERSHIP ISSUES

⊕ talkabout

1. What makes a good church leader?

⊕ investigate

❯ Read Titus 1 v 1-4

2. Who is the letter from (v 1) and to (v 4)?

3. What do verses 1-2 tell us about Paul's aim in his ministry? (**Note:** Verse 1 is better translated as the NIV 1984 does: "… an apostle of Jesus Christ for the faith of God's elect".)

• How does God make his eternal purposes and promises known (v 3)?

⊡ explore more

Paul describes Christians as "God's elect"—those God has chosen to give faith to so that they can be saved.

Why might the truth of God's election discourage us from evangelising?

▶ **Read Acts 18 v 5-11**

What effect did knowing that God had elected people in Corinth have on Paul?
So how does God's election encourage our evangelism?

⊖ apply

4. Why is evangelism eternally significant? How does this help us overcome our fears and do it?

5. Why are gospel churches the most important places in a town?

⊡ getting personal

The truth is that what you do for the gospel today has eternal implications. When you tell someone about Jesus, eternity is entering history. When someone becomes a Christian, that is an event with eternal implications. When you meet as church, it is the most significant event happening in your town.

How does this excite you today?

How should it change your priorities for your week?

⊕ investigate

❯ Read Titus 1 v 5-9

6. Why did Paul leave Titus in Crete (v 5)?

In verses 6-8, Paul focuses not on a leader's skills or experience, but on their home and character.

7. What should a leader's home life be like?

• What does this have to do with their church role (v 7a)?

8. What should a leader's character be like (both negatively and positively)?

• Take each one of these descriptions. What effect would it have on the church if a leader failed to have this character quality?

9. What else must a leader do (v 9)?

→ apply

10. In what situations would it be easy for church leaders not to fulfil the responsibilities of verse 9?

11. What makes a good church leader, and why does it matter?

12. How does this shape our own expectations of, and prayers for, our church leader(s)?

⊡ getting personal

Will you pray for your church leader(s) this week? When? What will you pray for them?

How do you think you could make your pastor's work more of a joy? (Perhaps you could ask them!)

⬆ pray

Thank God for:

• the eternal significance of gospel work.

• the church leaders he has given you.

Ask God to:

• enable your leaders to fit the description in verses 6-9.

• show you how you can encourage your leaders.

• help your leaders in any specific ways you know they or their families need.

2 Titus 1 v 10-16
HOW NOT TO GROW IN GODLINESS

The story so far

Paul's ministry shows nothing is more significant than gospel work. His command to Titus shows how important gospel-centred church leaders are.

⊕ talkabout

1. What are the biggest dangers to Christians successfully growing in godliness?

⊥ investigate

> **Read Titus 1 v 10-14**

2. Who does Paul identify as the "rebellious people" at the end of verse 10?

These teachers were a problem for the church in Galatia, too (Galatians 2 v 12).

3. **Read Galatians 4 v 17-18; 5 v 2-4.** What does the "circumcision group" seem to have been telling Christians in both Galatia and Crete?

4. What does Titus need to do with these people, and why (v 11)?

5. What does Titus need to do with those who are listening to them, and why (v 13-14)?

⊡ **getting personal**

How seriously do you take the issue of divisive teaching? Is there anyone you need to stop listening to; or anyone you need to warn?

In verse 10, Paul speaks of the circumcision group—people who say that to be godly, you must follow certain rules and rituals that are "human commands" (v 14). In verse 12, he says that those who live this way are still "liars, evil brutes, lazy gluttons". So they're very committed to following particular rules; yet they're also living very sinfully at the same time.

6. What does this show us about the shortcomings of a rule-based approach to godliness?

• **Read Colossians 2 v 20-23.** How does this add to your answer?

7. **Read Titus 1 v 1-2.** How has Paul already told us we can grow in godliness?

⊡ **explore more**

▶ **Read Luke 10 v 25-37**

What does the expert in the law want to know?
What is his motivation for asking? What does this reveal about his attitude to godliness?
How does Jesus' story force this man to stop limiting godliness by setting up rules about it?

⊖ **apply**

8. In what ways today do we find it tempting to reduce godliness to a list of do's and don'ts?

⊌ **investigate**

▶ **Read Titus 1 v 15-16**

9. What is true for pure people (ie: gospel-living Christians)? What is true for those who don't believe the gospel?

10. **Read Mark 7 v 20-23 and 1 Timothy 4 v 3-4.** Then take alcohol as an example. Alcohol itself is neither pure nor impure. What is it that makes drinking alcohol either "corrupt" or "pure"?

• Why is making a law that Christians must abstain from alcohol no better than abusing alcohol (1 Timothy 4 v 3-4)? What is the right way to approach it?

11. What, does Paul conclude, is the problem with making godliness all about following man-made rules (end of Titus 1 v 16)?

⮕ apply

12. Think about the following issues. How could we make the mistake of being legalistic (saying everyone must abstain) or of being licentious (saying everyone can do what they like) in each area? What would godliness look like?

• Playing computer games

- Watching romantic comedies

⊡ getting personal

Legalism says: *You should not do this because it's a sin.* The gospel says: *You need not do this because God is bigger and better than this sin.*

Think of a couple of sins you are struggling with. Are you seeking to resist them in a legalistic way, or in a gospel way? How can you preach gospel truth to yourself next time you're tempted?

⊕ pray

Thank God that there is a "truth that leads to godliness" (1 v 1). Praise him for ways in which you have seen each other growing in Christ-likeness; speak to him about ways in which you are struggling as individuals to live by the truth.

Confess to God any ways in which you have limited your view of godliness by reducing it to rules; or any ways in which you have been ignoring ungodliness in your life.

Ask God to give you wisdom about how to live in a godly way in areas where it is not immediately clear; and to give you such a love for him that you will live in a godly way in areas where it is difficult or costly to do so.

3 Titus 2 v 1-10
MAKING THE GOSPEL ATTRACTIVE

The story so far

Paul's ministry shows nothing is more significant than gospel work. His command to Titus shows how important gospel-centred church leaders are.

Titus needed to silence people who said Christians must add rules to faith to be saved; rules limit what godliness is, and have no power to motivate godly living.

⊕ talkabout

1. How can Christians live in a way that makes their faith attractive to others?

⊕ investigate

> **Read Titus 2 v 1**

2. What must Titus do (v 1)?

"Sound" means "healthy"—this is teaching that leads to spiritual and emotional health, to a good life characterised by good works.

⊳ Read Titus 2 v 2-10

3. What particular challenges and temptations do these verses suggest are faced by:
   • older men?

DICTIONARY

Temperate (v 2): showing self-restraint.
Reverent (v 3): respectful.
Be subject to (v 5, 9): follow the lead of.
Malign (v 5): speak badly of.

   • older women?

   • younger women?

   • younger men?

4. Verses 9-10 are addressed to slaves. But how does the teaching also apply to modern-day workers?

5. As well as teach, what must Titus make sure he does (v 7-8a)?

⊡ explore more

❱ Read Ephesians 5 v 21-28; 6 v 5-8; 1 Thessalonians 2 v 6-12

How do these verses give us extra details about how to live the good life, and why to live the good life, in the areas of:
- *marriage?*
- *work?*
- *church leadership?*

⊖ apply

6. How does this passage teach us to view those within our church who are:
- older than us?

- younger than us?

7. Imagine that in your own church each group mentioned here ignored Titus' teaching. What would it look like for them to do this in your context?

- Are there any of these that you think might be excused or go unchallenged by the rest of your church?

⊕ investigate

8. Each group needs to learn different things in particular. But two things need to be taught across the groups. What are they? What does each mean?

• v 2, 5, 6:

• v 5, 9:

9. As the members of the church, at their different stages of life and positions in society, live this way, what will happen, does Paul say?

• v 5b:

• v 8b:

• v 10b:

10. What do you make of this claim that self-control and submission make the gospel attractive (remember what kind of society Crete was, 1 v 12)?

⊟ apply

These verses outline the content of the good life which the gospel creates. But they also describe the context in which this life is to be shown, encouraged and lived—a church community, in which people are discipling each other.

11. As you see the kind of church community Titus is to form and lead in Crete, how does yours compare to this model?

- What might you start to do, or do more of (or less of!), to make your church more like this one?

⊡ getting personal

How will you be compellingly counter-cultural at home and/or at work this week?

⬆ pray

Thank God for giving you your church family.

Ask God to enable you to live as he wants, as the person he has made you, in the circumstances he's currently given you. And ask him to show you who you could teach, or who you could be taught by, or both, within your church community.

4 Titus 2 v 11-15
GRACE AND GLORY

The story so far

Paul's ministry shows nothing is more significant than gospel work. His command to Titus shows how important gospel-centred church leaders are.

Titus needed to silence people who said Christians must add rules to faith to be saved; rules limit what godliness is, and have no power to motivate godly living.

We face different challenges in our godly living depending on our age and stage; we can all live in self-controlled ways that make the gospel attractive.

⊕ talkabout

1. What motivations do people have for living in the way God wants?

• Which are good motivations, and which are not, do you think?

⊕ investigate

▶ **Read Titus 2 v 11-15**

2. What has appeared, and what is significant about that (v 11)? What event do you think Paul is referring to?

3. What will appear (v 13)?

4. What did the Jesus who *will* appear do when he *first* appeared (v 14)? Why?

5. What does Paul say Christians are waiting for (v 13)?

⊡ apply

6. How should knowing that we live between grace and glory shape our attitude towards:

• our mistakes?

• our regrets?

• the parts of life we find wonderful?

- the parts of life we find difficult?

7. How would it affect our attitudes and lives if we forgot either that God's grace has already appeared, or that God's glory will one day appear?

⊡ **investigate**

Jesus Christ came not only to redeem us, but to make us his people, "eager to do what is good" (v 14).

8. What does God's grace teach us to do in life (v 12)? What do each of these phrases/words mean?

The question is: How does God's grace teach us to do these things? Because it changes the way we see our future, our love, and ourselves.

9. How do God's grace and glory change:
  • our view of our future (and therefore our present) (v 13)?

  • how we love (v 14a; see 1 John 4 v 19)?

  • how we see ourselves (v 14b)?

  • How do each of these teach us to live in the way verse 12 says?

10. What is Titus to do with this truth (v 15)? What should we want our own church leaders to do with this?

⊡ getting personal

Legalism says: *What we do leads to who we are.* The gospel tells us: *What we are leads to what we do.* You are part of the people who Christ died to make "his very own".

So how will you be "eager to do what is good" this week? What "good" are you being called to do, that is costly or inconvenient?

⊡ explore more

optional

▶ Read Hebrews 11 v 24-26

How is Moses a great example of the way in which grace teaches us to live in our present?
What would it mean for you to live like Moses in your culture and context?

⊝ apply

11. What motivations does this passage give us for living the way God wants?

12. Take a couple of areas where all or several of you find Christian obedience hard. How does this passage shape your thinking about those areas?

⬆ pray

Take each part of verses 11 and 13-14 in turn, praising God for the truths about him that they contain.

Then use verses 12 and 14-15 to ask God for his help in living a "good life" that is motivated by past grace and future glory.

If you are comfortable doing so, share ways in which you are personally struggling to say "no" to ungodliness, and then pray for each other.

5 Titus 3 v 1-15
STRESS THESE THINGS

The story so far

Titus needed to silence people who said Christians must add rules to faith to be saved; rules limit what godliness is, and have no power to motivate godly living.

We face different challenges in our godly living depending on our age and stage; we can all live in self-controlled ways that make the gospel attractive.

Christ's past coming in grace, and future coming in glory, teach us that we are his people, making us eager to say "no" to ungodliness and do what is good.

⊕ talkabout

1. How do you think of God? What words do you use to describe him?

⊕ investigate

> **Read Titus 3 v 1-8a**

2. What uncomfortable truths about ourselves do we discover in verse 3?

DICTIONARY

Righteous (v 5): good.
Mercy (v 5): an act of not giving someone the punishment they deserve.
Justified (v 7): declared not guilty, completely innocent.

Remember, "appeared" is Paul's phrase for the coming of God's salvation in Jesus.

3. How is this appearing described here (v 4-5a)?

4. Why did God save us (v 5)?

5. What is the Holy Spirit's role in saving us?

🙂 getting personal

Verse 6 tells us that God measures out the Spirit to us in accordance with what his Son deserves—it comes to us "through Jesus". How much do you think that is? How much do you think Jesus is worth to God? The Spirit has been poured out "generously"—not like a cup of water, but like a waterfall.

How much do you expect the Spirit to be at work in your life?

The answer depends on how much you think the death of Jesus is worth to his Father.

6. How do these verses help us to "measure" the kindness and love of God?

⊟ apply

7. Share with your group which truth about God's kindness particularly thrills you today.

8. How do verses 3-5 prevent us feeling:
- proud?

- worthless or hopeless?

⊡ investigate

> ❯ **Read Titus 3 v 1-2, 8b-15**

9. What should Titus:
- remind his church (v 1-2)?

<table>
<tr><td>DICTIONARY</td></tr>
</table>

**Profitable (v 8)/
unprofitable (v 9):** helpful/
unhelpful.
Genealogies (v 9): lists of
people's ancestors.
Self-condemned (v 11):
proving themselves to be
guilty.
Apollos (v 13): a prominent
and popular church leader.

- stress to his church (v 8)?

• avoid (v 9)?

10. Why do you think Paul uses such strong language in verses 10-11 (think about the letter as a whole)?

optional

⊞ explore more

What does Paul want Titus to do for Apollos and Zenas (v 13)?

❯ Read 1 Corinthians 1 v 11-12

Why might Paul have been tempted to hinder, or at best not to help, Apollos in his ministry? What is impressive about Titus 3 v 13?

❯ Read 1 Corinthians 3 v 1-9

What truths about ministry meant that Paul wanted to support Apollos, not compete with him?

⤇ apply

11. Why do we often find ourselves focusing on disagreements and quarrels, rather than the gospel?

12. How, practically, can we "stress these things"—that is, the content of verses 3-8a—in our conversations and lives?

⬆ **pray**

Thank God for...

Confess to God...

Ask God...

The good life

LEADER'S GUIDE

Leader's Guide

INTRODUCTION

Leading a Bible study can be a bit like herding cats—everyone has a different idea of what the passage could be about, and a different line of enquiry that they want to pursue. But a good group leader is more than someone who just referees this kind of discussion. You will want to:

- correctly understand and handle the Bible passage. But also…

- encourage and train the people in your group to do this for themselves. Don't fall into the trap of spoon-feeding people by simply passing on the information in the Leader's Guide. Then…

- make sure that no Bible study is finished without everyone knowing how the passage is relevant for them. What changes do you all need to make in the light of the things you have been learning? And finally…

- encourage the group to turn all that has been learned and discussed into prayer.

Your Bible-study group is unique, and you are likely to know better than anyone the capabilities, backgrounds and circumstances of the people you are leading. That's why we've designed these guides with a number of optional features. If they're a quiet bunch, you might want to spend longer on talkabout. If your time is limited, you can choose to skip explore more, or get people to look at these questions at home. Can't get enough of Bible study? Well, some studies have optional extra homework projects. As leader, you can adapt and select the material to the needs of your particular group.

So what's in the Leader's Guide? The main thing that this Leader's Guide will help you to do is to understand the major teaching points in the passage you are studying, and how to apply them. As well as guidance on the questions, the Leader's Guide for each session contains the following important sections:

THE BIG IDEA

One or two key sentences will give you the main point of the session. This is what you should be aiming to have fixed in people's minds as they leave the Bible study. And it's the point you need to head back towards when the discussion goes off at a tangent.

SUMMARY

An overview of the passage, including plenty of useful historical background information.

OPTIONAL EXTRA

Usually this is an introductory activity that ties in with the main theme of the Bible study, and is designed to "break the ice" at the beginning of a session. Or it may be a "homework project" that people can tackle during the week.

So let's take a look at the various different features of a Good Book Guide:

⊕ talkabout

Each session kicks off with a discussion question, based on the group's opinions or experiences. It's designed to get people talking and thinking in a general way about the main subject of the Bible study.

⬇ investigate

The first thing you and your group need to know is what the Bible passage is about, which is the purpose of these questions. But watch out—people may come up with answers based on their experiences or teaching they have heard in the past, without referring to the passage at all. It's amazing how often we can get through a Bible study without actually looking at the Bible! If you're stuck for an answer, the Leader's Guide contains guidance on questions. These are the answers to direct your group to. This information isn't meant to be read out to people—ideally, you want them to discover these answers from the Bible for themselves. Sometimes there are optional follow-up questions (see ☑ in guidance on questions) to help you help your group get to the answer.

⬡ explore more

These questions generally point people to other relevant parts of the Bible. They are useful for helping your group to see how the passage fits into the "big picture" of the whole Bible. These sections are OPTIONAL—only use them if you have time. Remember that it's better to finish in good time having really grasped one big thing from the passage, than to try and cram everything in.

➔ apply

We want to encourage you to spend more time working at application—too often, it is simply tacked on at the end. In the Good Book Guides, apply sections are mixed in with the investigate sections of the study. We hope that people will realise that application is not just an optional extra, but rather, the whole purpose of studying the

Bible. We do Bible study so that our lives can be changed by what we hear from God's word. If you skip the application, the Bible study hasn't achieved its purpose.

These questions draw out practical lessons that we can all learn from the Bible passage. You can review what has been learned so far, and think about practical differences that this should make in our churches and our lives. The group gets the opportunity to talk about what they personally have learned.

⊡ getting personal

These can be done at home, but it is well worth allowing a few moments of quiet reflection during the study for each person to think and pray about specific changes they need to make in their own lives. Why not have a time for reporting back at the beginning of the following session, so that everyone can be encouraged and challenged by one another to make application a priority?

⬆ pray

In Acts 4 v 25-30 the first Christians quoted Psalm 2 as they prayed in response to the persecution of the apostles by the Jewish religious leaders. Today however, it's not as common for Christians to base prayers on the truths of God's word as it once was. As a result, our prayers tend to be weak, superficial and self-centered rather than bold, visionary and God-centered.

The prayer section is based on what has been learned from the Bible passage. How different our prayer times would be if we were genuinely responding to what God has said to us through his word!

1 Titus 1 v 1-9
LEADERSHIP ISSUES

THE BIG IDEA
Nothing is more significant than gospel work and gospel churches; so having leaders who are godly in the home, in character and in doctrine is vital.

SUMMARY
Paul begins by describing the nature of his ministry as a servant of the church (which Titus also is), as well as an apostle (v 1-3). His aim is to bring God's people to faith, and then equip them to grow in godliness (v 1). This is of eternal importance, because the gospel looks back to God's promise of eternal life, made "before the beginning of time", and looks forward to "the hope of eternal life" (v 2). And this eternal life is brought to light in preaching (v 3).

In writing to Titus (v 4), Paul is concerned with the issue of succession. He wants to ensure that Titus is equipped for the task of church leadership, and that there are other leaders to take care of the church who will be faithful to the gospel message and the gospel task. Titus is to "appoint elders" (v 5)—and he is to choose men who are "blameless" (ie: above reproach, rather than totally perfect):
- in the home (v 6)
- in character (v 7-8)
- in doctrine (v 9)

So this study teaches us both the significance of evangelism and the local church; and the vital importance of godly leadership in the church.

OPTIONAL EXTRA
Verses 5-9 are a "job description" of a church elder, or leader. From a local newspaper, cut out a variety of job adverts, and cut off the job title, leaving just the list of desirable qualifications and abilities. Ask your group to guess from the job description what each job is. If you have time, you could mock up a "job advert" for church elder, and put that in with the other ads from your local paper.

GUIDANCE FOR QUESTIONS
1. What makes a good church leader?
Many things! At this point, just let your group make suggestions, without discussing them too much or rejecting those you feel aren't right. Make sure answers range beyond: "Teaching the Bible well". You'll return to this question in Q11.

2. Who is the letter from (v 1) and to (v 4)? From Paul (v 1), an apostle (a witness to Jesus whose teaching comes with Jesus' authority).
To Titus (v 4), a younger man who was a protégé of Paul's (his "son in our common faith"). If you have time, your group can discover more about Titus in 2 Corinthians 8 v 16-24.

3. What do verses 1-2 tell us about Paul's aim in his ministry? (Note: Verse 1 is better translated as the NIV 84 does: "… an apostle of Jesus Christ for the faith of God's elect".)
- His first goal was to bring to saving faith those whom God had chosen to be saved (the elect). Paul knew that God had chosen to save some, and so he preached

the gospel to all, knowing that those God had chosen would respond with faith (see Explore More on Acts 18 v 5-11). **Note:** Don't get sidetracked into a discussion on election here. The important point is that Paul's aim was to evangelise, so that people would come to faith.

- Secondly, Paul laboured to ensure Christians would grow in the faith—grow in "godliness" (v 1)—by growing in their knowledge of the truth (ie: the gospel).

- **How does God make his eternal purposes and promises known (v 3)?** "Through the preaching entrusted to me." Eternal life is "brought to light" through gospel preaching. Eternal life appears in our towns when we talk about Jesus.

EXPLORE MORE
Why might the truth of God's election discourage us from evangelising? Since God has already chosen whom to save, our evangelism won't save someone whom he hasn't chosen; and he'll save someone he has chosen, even if we don't evangelise. **Read Acts 18 v 5-11. What effect did knowing that God had elected people in Corinth have on Paul?** Verse 11: He stayed there for a year and a half, preaching the word of God.
So how does God's election encourage our evangelism? We know there are people out there whom God has chosen to bring to faith and life. All they need is for someone to preach the gospel—that someone could be you or me! The main thing that stops me witnessing to Christ is the feeling that it will probably be a waste of time. But since we can't tell who God's elect are, it is never a waste of time! That person we could talk about Jesus with could be someone whom God will bring to faith through our words.

4. APPLY: Why is evangelism eternally significant? How does this help us overcome our fears and do it? As we speak the gospel, eternity enters history. Christ is made present as we speak. People meet Jesus in our words. And when someone becomes a Christian, that is a bigger event in eternal terms than the brightest cosmic explosion. And sharing the gospel is the means God uses to bring his people to faith. So our evangelism is never powerless or pointless (which are two of our biggest fears that stop us speaking to people about Jesus).

5. APPLY: Why are gospel churches the most important places in a town? Because they are where the people God chose before eternity, and who will live with him eternally, are gathered. They are also the places where people can come on a Sunday and, through preaching, see Christ and see eternity. We can often feel small, marginalised and inconsequential; but the local church is part of God's eternal purposes, the place where things of eternal significance happen.

6. Why did Paul leave Titus in Crete (v 5)? To finish what Paul had left unfinished, by putting it "in order"—in other words, by appointing elders "in every town", ie: in each congregation. Paul had preached the gospel, founded the church and begun to disciple the new believers; but he'd left before he had been able to appoint elders, or church leaders.

7. What should a leader's home life be like?
- Blameless (v 6): this doesn't mean entirely without fault, but rather to have a good reputation, against which no fair accusation can be made.

- "Faithful to his wife": a one-woman man. This does not exclude single men; but it means that, if married, their marriage must be strong and faithful and committed.
- "A man whose children believe": "children" here implies small children. The beliefs of young children reflect what they are taught and modelled at home. So an elder should be intentionally teaching the gospel to his children at home, and exerting loving discipline rather than letting his children be "wild and disobedient".
- **What does this have to do with their church role (v 7a)?** The church is God's "household"—his family—and so an elder is managing God's family. The way a man leads his own family reveals a lot about how he will lead God's family. So if a man cannot lead his own family well, he should not be given the responsibility of leading God's family.

8. What should a leader's character be like (both negatively and positively)?
Not (v 7):
- overbearing: he must not be dominating or controlling.
- quick-tempered: he needs to be patient, able to listen well and think calmly.
- given to drunkenness, not violent: these show a lack of self-control, which is one of an elder's "must-haves" (v 8).
- pursuing dishonest gain: elders must be motivated by unselfish love, rather than the desire to gain popularity or wealth or status for themselves.
He must (v 8):
- be hospitable: willing to open up his home and life, and give his time, to others.
- love what is good: the whole of Titus is written to encourage Titus to model and teach the church to "devote themselves to doing what is good" (3 v 8); that is, "what is appropriate to sound doctrine" (2 v 1).

Elders need to love godliness if they are going to be men who model and teach it.
- be self-controlled.
- be upright, holy and disciplined: in other words, godly in morality, and committed to living that way.
Paul's primary concern is not finding the people with the best skills. His primary concern is with character.

☒
- **Why do you think Paul is more concerned with character than gifts?**
  - Skills used for selfish ends become destructive. The tyrants of this world are very gifted; but they bring misery because their aims are selfish.
  - Truth failure normally starts with moral failure. If we are not living obediently in a part of life, soon enough we will change our beliefs and teaching to excuse our behaviour. In a leader, this is catastrophic for a church, as well as for themselves and their family.

- **Take each one of these descriptions. What effect would it have on the church if a leader failed to have this character quality?** If you do not have much time, ask your group to pick out three or four of the "must nots" or "must bes" and think through the consequences of being the opposite. Eg: if a leader is overbearing, he will not delegate or allow others to use their gifts; he is likely to be harsh and proud; his congregation will either resent him or have an unhealthy reliance on him; he will probably not listen to criticism; etc.

9. What else must a leader do (v 9)? Hold firmly to "the trustworthy message as it has been taught", ie: to the teaching of the apostles in the New Testament, based on the Old Testament Scriptures—that is, the gospel (notice Paul mentions that 3 v 3-7 is a "trustworthy teaching" in v 8a). This involves: (1) encouraging the church through teaching apostolic truth; (2) opposing those who don't hold to apostolic truth.

10. APPLY: In what situations would it be easy for church leaders not to fulfil the responsibilities of verse 9? There are two opposite errors: under-pastoring (where leaders don't refute error) and over-pastoring (where leaders dominate).
The first often happens when leaders fear the rejection of others (church members or the wider community) more than they fear God. It is difficult and costly and often exhausting to refute error or confront difficult situations.
The second often happens when leaders are trying to prove themselves, or need to feel in control. It may come out when a mistake has been made; or when the possibility of delegating leadership roles to others is raised; or when a criticism is made.

11. APPLY: What makes a good church leader, and why does it matter? This is referring back to Q1. A good church leader is one whose home, character and commitment to the gospel match up to Paul's list in verses 6-9. It is worth underlining that Paul sees these aspects as more important than the elder's gifts. It matters because the church matters; it is where Christ is made clear in our neighbourhoods, and it is God's family. An overseer "manages God's household" (v 7). It is hard to over-estimate how much good, godly leadership of churches matters.

12. APPLY: How does this shape our own expectations of, and prayers for, our church leader(s)? It is good to prioritise what Paul does. We often exalt our pastors' preaching abilities, or sense of humour, or intellectual insight as more important than the kind of husbands and/or fathers they are; whether they will humbly but firmly oppose error; whether they are hospitable; and so on. It is worth comparing your list from Q1 with your list in Q11, to see how they match up and how your expectations might need to change.
And, having seen the importance of church and an elder's role within church, we'll pray for them!

2 Titus 1 v 10-16
HOW NOT TO GROW IN GODLINESS

THE BIG IDEA
Rules limit godliness, and have no power to grow us in godliness. We need to silence legalism, and use the gospel to motivate our godly living.

SUMMARY
One reason why Titus needs to appoint elders who will teach the truth is that "rebellious people" have arisen (v 10)—disorder has entered the church. These people must be "silenced", because they are disrupting "whole households"—ie: churches meeting in homes (v 11).

Paul appears to have in mind two groups of people—the disruptive teachers (v 10-11), and those who have come under their influence (v 13-14). The former need silencing, as much as possible; the latter need warning and rebuking, so that they will be influenced to grow in gospel truth.

Why does this matter so much? Because, although we do not know what these false teachers were teaching, they were "of the circumcision group". Galatians 2 v 12; 4 v 17-18; 5 v 2-4 describes these teachers as claiming that Christians need to obey rules (being circumcised, Jewish law, etc) in order to remain, or grow, as Christians. They are "legalists". Paul tells Titus that in fact, this group are not encouraging godliness; they are limiting it. They are still like the worst of Cretans (Titus 1 v 12). They obey certain rules, but ignore ungodliness in other areas. Legalism limits godliness.

Secondly, legalism has no power to produce godliness. Though these teachers "claim to know God ... by their actions they deny him" (v 16). Their teaching does not produce "anything good", because simply imposing a rule does not motivate godly living. It is the truth of the gospel that is the only real fuel for godliness (v 1).

This means that we need to avoid legalism ("you must live this way") as much as we need to avoid licentiousness ("live how you want"). All things are created by God as good, and can be enjoyed according to his word, giving thanks to him. "To the pure, all things are pure" (v 15), because they are enjoyed in a pure way. Q12 picks up on some practical applications for this approach (you may wish to substitute other areas that are more relevant to your particular group).

OPTIONAL EXTRA
In verse 12, Paul quotes one of Crete's own "prophets", who describes Cretans in a very negative way! Get your group to describe people in their town in five words, positively. Then ask them to do it negatively. And then do the same for your state or country.

GUIDANCE FOR QUESTIONS
1. What are the biggest dangers to Christians successfully growing in godliness? You may need to define what is meant by "godliness"—growing to be more like God. So another phrase is "Christ-likeness", since Jesus is the image of the invisible God. Romans 8 v 28-29 tells us that God's purpose in our lives is for us to be "conformed to the image of his Son".

There are no "wrong answers" at this point—you could refer back to this question at the end of the study. The surprising answer these verses gives is that following rules is a danger to true godliness.

2. Who does Paul identify as the "rebellious people" at the end of verse 10? "The circumcision group." **(Note:** "Especially" should probably be translated "that is". Paul is not saying the circumcision group are a particularly rebellious part of a larger rebellious group; he is identifying them as the rebellious ones.)

3. These teachers were a problem for the church in Galatia, too (Gal 2 v 12). Read Galatians 4 v 17-18; 5 v 2-4. What does the "circumcision group" seem to have been telling Christians in both Galatia and Crete? "You become a Christian by faith in Christ—but to stay a Christian, or grow as a Christian, or be a proper Christian, you need to be circumcised." They wanted to make non-Jewish Christians subject to the Jewish law, or to a human code of conduct (see Titus 1 v 14). Galatians 5 v 4 shows that they were teaching that you begin as a Christian by God's grace, his undeserved kindness and mercy; but you stay justified not by grace, but by keeping God's law.

4. What does Titus need to do with these people, and why (v 11)? Silence them—stop them from speaking in the churches, etc—because they are disrupting whole households with their teaching. First-century churches met in homes; so "households" is Paul's way of referring to church gatherings.

5. What does Titus need to do with those who are listening to them, and why (v 12-14)? Rebuke them sharply. That is, tell them off, tell them they are wrong to listen to these false teachers, so that they will "be sound in the faith" (v 13). Notice that Paul has two groups of people in mind. First, there are those who "reject the truth" (v 14), the "circumcision group", who have rejected the Christian faith. These men must be silenced. But the other group are those Christians who are mistakenly listening to and being influenced by the first group—they need to be rebuked and brought back to listen to the gospel.

6. What does this [Paul saying that the circumcision group (v 10) are "liars, evil brutes, lazy gluttons" (v 12)] show us about the shortcomings of a rule-based approach to godliness? It doesn't work, for two reasons.
1. Rules that look as if they are about promoting godliness actually limit godliness. They reduce a whole life pursuit of Christ-likeness to ticking some boxes (Have you been circumcised? Do you keep the festival days? Do you read your Bible each day? Do you do street evangelism? etc). So in Crete, the circumcision group would say to a circumcised glutton: *You're godly.* So when we have a rule-based approach to godliness, we end up ignoring ungodliness in other areas where we haven't imposed rules.
2. Verse 16: "They claim to know God, but by their actions they deny him. They are … unfit for doing anything good." We can impose rules on ourselves or others; but we can't keep them. Rules don't give us any power or motivation to live in a godly way.

- **Read Colossians 2 v 20-23. How does this add to your answer?** Paul says explicitly here what Titus 1 v 10-16 suggests—that though living by a set of rules seems wise, worship-minded and humble, "they lack any value in restraining sensual indulgence" (v 23). Simply saying to someone (or ourselves): "You should not do this" or "You should do that" doesn't give us any motive or power to obey.

7. Read Titus 1 v 1-2. How has Paul already told us we can grow in godliness? It is "knowledge of the truth" that leads to godliness (v 1). That "truth" is the gospel—the certain hope of eternal life, promised by God. The more we know who God is, what he has done for us, what lies ahead of us, and who we therefore are as children of God, the more we will want to live for God and be like God in every area of our lives. This is the real engine for godliness.

EXPLORE MORE
Read Luke 10 v 25-37. What does the expert in the law want to know?
• v 25: "What must I do to inherit eternal life?"
• v 29: "Who is my neighbour?" (ie: who do I need to love as much as I love myself?)
What is his motivation for asking? What does this reveal about his attitude to godliness? "He wanted to justify himself" (v 29). The problem is not his question, but his motivation—he wanted to know what he needed to do so that he could ensure he was good enough for God. His question is: *What is the minimal requirement that will enable me to get eternal life?* He wants a specific law to limit what godliness involves.
How does Jesus' story force this man to stop limiting godliness by setting up rules about it? By showing him that absolutely everyone is his neighbour—including a Samaritan, whom this Jewish legal expert would naturally consider an

enemy—and that therefore to love your neighbour is to be willing to give absolutely everything you have for your enemy. Jesus is radically expanding the scope of loving your neighbour—and he's saying: *To love your neighbour as yourself means loving everyone in the way that I love them.* So the expert in the law needs to be like Christ. That's the standard of godliness.

8. APPLY: In what ways today do we find it tempting to reduce godliness to a list of do's and don'ts? One way to get at how we do this is to ask: *How can we grow as Christians?* Most of us reduce the answer to a checklist: *Do read your Bible, Do go to church, Don't get drunk,* and so on. These are all good things to do and not do; but if that's our view of godliness, we've limited it.

9. What is true for pure people (ie: gospel-living Christians)? "All things are pure." **What is true for those who don't believe the gospel?** "Nothing is pure."

10. Read Mark 7 v 20-23 and 1 Timothy 4 v 3-4. Then take alcohol as an example. Alcohol itself is neither pure nor impure. What is it that makes drinking alcohol either "corrupt" or "pure"? The way in which we use it. If we use alcohol in a sinful or selfish way, then it isn't pure. Alcohol itself does not corrupt us; our hearts are corrupt (Mark 7 v 20-23), so we use things in a way that is corrupt. But 1 Timothy 4 v 3-4 says that everything was made by God, and is to be enjoyed in its proper way, with thanksgiving.

• **Why is making a law that Christians must abstain from alcohol no better than abusing alcohol (1 Timothy 4 v 3-4)?** Because that law would be denying that alcohol is part of God's creation. It would be saying that godliness must mean denying that something that is "good" is good. **What is the right way to approach it?** 1 Timothy 4 v 3-4 says that we are free to enjoy alcohol as a good gift of God, and use it for his glory in accordance with his word, by not drinking to excess, and drinking thankfully.

Note: That is not to say that an individual who struggles with alcohol is wrong to give up drinking altogether. But it would be wrong for them to decide that everyone should stop drinking because they think that's the only "godly" thing to do.

11. What, does Paul conclude, is the problem with making godliness all about following man-made rules (end of Titus 1 v 16)? It doesn't work! We say we are following the rules and are godly, but our "actions ... deny" God. We will either ignore ungodliness in other areas of our lives, or simply break our rules and seek excuses for doing so—because rules don't give any motivation for obedience.

12. APPLY: Think about the following issues. How could we make the mistake of being legalistic (saying everyone must abstain) or of being licentious (saying everyone can do what they like) in each area? What would godliness look like?
• **Playing computer games**
Legalistic: Computer games are bad. They can lead to addiction, or time-wasting, or aggression. Christians should not play computer games; it is ungodly.
Licentious: Computer games are good. There is nothing wrong with them; so it's never a problem to play them.
Godly: Computer games can be enjoyed for the glory of God, in accordance with his word, as a good gift from him. They are not always bad. But equally, if they

are becoming something that dominates my thinking or time or emotions, then the godly thing to do is probably to get rid of them.

• **Watching romantic comedies**
Legalistic: Rom-coms encourage people to be discontented; and they present an unrealistic and even immoral view of relationships. Therefore rom-coms are bad; godly Christians will avoid them.
Licentious: Rom-coms are fun and if you like them, there's no problem with watching them.
Godly: Rom-coms are not intrinsically bad. If you can watch them and enjoy them as a good gift from God, without being discontent, then that's fine. But if your corrupt heart responds to them with discontent or some other sin, then they might be best avoided.

3 Titus 2 v 1-10
MAKING THE GOSPEL ATTRACTIVE

THE BIG IDEA

We have different roles to play in our church community, depending on our age and stage of life. But all of us are to be self-controlled and submissive, in a way that is counter-cultural but attracts our culture to the gospel.

SUMMARY

In this section, Paul tells Titus what he needs to teach people in his churches, at various stages of life, so that they can teach each other, and in this way grow in godliness. He's to "teach ... sound doctrine" (v 1). "Sound" means "healthy"—this is teaching that will lead people to a healthy life, or a good life, characterised by good works.

Paul gives different instructions for different categories of people—older men, older women, younger women, younger men and slaves (today, we can see this category as employees). This assumes that different ages and different roles face different challenges and temptations. And the older Christians are to teach the younger Christians. This is profoundly counter-cultural—we tend to choose the new thing over the old thing. As Christians, we need to act as father or mother figures (if we're older), or look for those figures (if we're younger).

Two qualities are repeated as necessary for different groups: self-control (v 2, v 5, v 6) and submission (v 5, v 9). Again, these are qualities our culture rejects; yet Paul says that living this way "will make the teaching about God our Saviour attractive" (v 10).

People may not like it when we talk about self-control and submission; but they will find it attractive when we live it. Today, we need people in our churches to be "acting our age"—teaching and learning from each other, and encouraging one another to live in a way that is counter-cultural but compelling to our culture, making the gospel attractive to those around us by our conduct.

OPTIONAL EXTRA

Divide a large piece of paper into four quarters. On the top of the left-hand column, write "Older". On top of the right-hand column, write "Younger". Then to the left of the top row, write "Good things" and to the left of the bottom row, "Less good things". Then get your group to fill it in, thinking of the positives and negatives of being an older person and a younger person. The make-up of your church membership will dictate what you see as "older" and "younger"—in one church, "older" may be anyone over 35; in another, "younger" may be anyone under 50. Encourage your group to think of qualities that older and younger people tend to have; and particular challenges they tend to face. You could refer back to your sheet, and add to it, as you answer Q3.

GUIDANCE FOR QUESTIONS

1. How can Christians live in a way that makes their faith attractive to others? Many ways! Take suggestions, and don't allow the discussion to continue for too long. You can come back to this question after Q9 or Q10 to see the surprising way Paul answers this question in this passage.

2. What must Titus do (v 1)? Teach sound doctrine.

3. What particular challenges and temptations do these verses suggest are faced by: (You can answer this by seeing what each group needs to be taught, and thinking about what that group's specific temptations therefore seem to have been.)

- **older men?** Being grumpy, picking arguments, being cynical, becoming tired of serving sacrificially.

- **older women?** "Likewise" (v 3) suggests they face similar temptations to men of the same age. But they are also facing the temptation of being gossips and criticising others ("They're not the wives/mothers/ daughters they should be"; "Things were different when I was in their position", etc); and the temptation to self-indulgence and excess.

- **younger women?** For wives and mothers, the challenge must have been to focus on loving their family and see this as their primary way of serving; for all younger women, there is a temptation not to guard purity (whether single or married); and for those who are married, allowing their husband to lead is not always very easy.

- **younger men?** They receive only one word of exhortation (v 6)! They need to be self-controlled. But that does cover the temptations younger guys face—lust, ambition and impatience all require a response of self-control.

4. Verses 9-10 are addressed to slaves. But how does the teaching also apply to modern-day workers? Instead of doing what is required and no more, workers should try to please their bosses. They should accept that they are not the boss, and submit humbly to the boss's authority. And rather than seeking to "take" what we can get away with at work (perhaps an extra five minutes at lunch, etc), we should be utterly trustworthy. This requires not simply a set of rules to keep as a worker, but a radically different attitude, where we seek to be proactive in blessing our masters.

5. As well as teach, what must Titus make sure he does (v 7-8a)? He is to set an example. The way he lives and the manner of his teaching need to match the content of his teaching. He is to model the impact of God's grace in his life, as he tells others how God's grace should be at work in their lives.

EXPLORE MORE
Read Ephesians 5 v 21-28; 6 v 5-8; 1 Thessalonians 2 v 6-12. How do these verses give us extra details about how to live the good life, and why to live the good life, in the areas of:
- **marriage?** Wives are to submit to their husbands as the church does to Christ, ie: loyally following their lead, letting them take the decisions, and loving them exclusively.
Husbands are to love their wives as Christ loves the church, ie: giving up what is easiest or most comfortable for themselves in order to do what is best for their wife; always considering their wife's faith and godliness as a priority; being willing to die for their wife.
- **work?** Again, these words are addressed to slaves, but there is much for workers today to learn. We're to treat our masters as we treat Christ, in humble obedience

(v 5); we're to remember that ultimately we're working for Christ, and so do what is right when we're not being watched as well as when we are (v 6); and we're to remember that the Lord will reward good living, and see our work as a way of serving him (v 7-8).

- **church leadership?** This picks up on Paul's words to Titus in Titus 2 v 7-8a. Paul did not seek people's approval (v 6); he cared about this young church as a mother does her young children (v 7-8); he shared his life with them, as well as teaching them, because he loved them (v 8); he did this even though it made his life harder (v 9); and his life was a model to them of the grace-shaped life (v 10) as he encouraged them to live that life too (v 11-12).

6. APPLY: How does this passage teach us to view those within our church who are:

- **older than us?** We should respect them and seek to be taught by them. There is a proper authority that goes with age; and when we are younger, we need to be fathered or mothered by those who are older than us, who have more experience of life and of living by faith (just as Titus appears to have viewed Paul, 1 v 4).

- **younger than us?** We should make sure we are worthy of their respect; and make ourselves available to share life with those who are younger, to listen and advise and teach. Instead of criticising mistakes, we should teach how to live well.

7. APPLY: Imagine that in your own church each group mentioned here ignored Titus' teaching. What would it look like for them to do this in your context? In Crete, it looked like 1 v 12. But each culture is different, and so the damage caused by ignoring this kind of teaching will look different. We'll be tempted to (for instance) slander others in different ways; or to be impure or not self-controlled in different ways.

- **Are there any of these that you think might be excused or go unchallenged by the rest of your church?** We all have blind spots—sins we don't notice, or sins that we make excuses about on others' behalf. Again, these will vary from context to context—it could be getting drunk when it's in your own home; or flirting; or harshness of tone among the elderly. This is a chance for your group to think about what they might not notice as being unhelpful/sinful; or where they might not teach others well because they don't think that a particular weakness really matters.

8. Each group needs to learn different things in particular. But two things need to be taught across the groups. What are they? What does each mean?

- **v 2, 5, 6:** Self-control. This does not mean to be self-repressed, or not to be emotional; it means to have our emotions and actions under control, directed by the gospel rather than dominating us. Eg: anger without self-control pursues revenge or self-vindication; self-controlled anger pursues justice and mercy.

- **v 5, 9:** Submission. God has made a world that contains authority. He is the supreme authority; and he delegates authority in different areas to particular people (state authorities; elders in church; husbands in the home; bosses/masters in the workplace). Submission is not about never having an opinion or speaking up. It is about recognising authority, and submitting to it humbly and joyfully, unless and until it would be ungodly to do so.

9. As the members of the church, at their different stages of life and positions in society, live this way, what will happen, does Paul say?

• **v 5b:** No one will malign (criticise) God's word.

• **v 8b:** Opponents will be ashamed, because there is nothing that deserves being opposed.

• **v 10b:** Gospel teaching will be attractive.

10. What do you make of this claim that self-control and submission make the gospel attractive (remember what kind of society Crete was, 1 v 12)?
Self-control and submission would have been very counter-cultural to people in a society that tolerated lying, evil, laziness and gluttony! It is not that when the church spoke of self-control or submission, their surrounding culture was ready to agree with that teaching. But Paul is saying that people will find that way of living attractive when they see it. The same is true today. The Christian life is counter-cultural, but it is also compelling. Unbelievers who are repelled by Christian teaching on headship within marriage, or Christian morality, are attracted by the Christian marriages they see, and by the loving Christians they know. The way we live will make what we teach attractive.

11. APPLY: As you see the kind of church community Titus is to form and lead in Crete, how does yours compare to this model?
• **What might you start to do, or do more of (or less of!) to make your church more like this one?**
Don't allow your discussion here to become critical or harsh about your church leadership (remember Study One). Notice that Titus is not being told to set up any groups, or a discipleship programme; he's to teach and model the godly, good life to his church, and they are then to live it and teach it to each other. So your group can all apply this teaching to each other, and to their church relationships, without needing someone else to set up a programme or structure. It is a community-based, organic discipleship that Paul is telling Titus to model and teach.

4 Titus 2 v 11-15
GRACE AND GLORY

THE BIG IDEA
God's past coming in grace and future coming in glory teach us that we are his people, and make us eager to say "no" to ungodliness and to do what is good.

SUMMARY
In 2 v 1-10, Paul described the content of the good life Titus was to teach his church to live—now in these verses, he describes the source of this good life. "These … are the things [he] should teach" (v 15). Here we find the motivation for living the life God wants us to.

In the original Greek, v 11-14 is all one sentence. Paul says we live between two "appearings". Verse 11: "the grace of God appeared" (past tense). This was the first "coming" of Jesus, to give himself for us and redeem us (v 14). Now, verse 13, we wait for "the appearing of … glory" (future), when Jesus will return in all God's power and majesty. (V 13 refers to God the Father, whose glory will appear in the future—and that glory is Jesus Christ. So we can read it as: "the appearing of the glory of our great God and Saviour [the Father], [and the glory of God the Father is] Jesus Christ".)

So verse 12 tells us what grace teaches us, as we live between the appearing of God's grace in Christ, and the appearing of God's glory in Christ. Grace shapes our lives in the present, as well as preparing us for Christ's return. How? In three ways:

- It changes our hope—we now have a "blessed hope" (v 13), so we look forward to that and say "no" to ungodliness (a word used to describe worshipping something other than God, see Romans 1 v 18). Grace teaches us that God is better, fuller and richer than anything else that we could love or serve. We place our hopes in him.
- It changes our love. Because we know Jesus gave himself for us, his love wins our hearts and we love to serve him and obey him (see also 1 John 4 v 19).
- It changes our identity. Verse 14 tells us that Jesus died to make us "a people that are his very own, eager to do what is good". Our identity is as God's children, Christ's people—so we want to live in a way that matches who we are.

OPTIONAL EXTRA

Paul teaches in these verses that waiting for glory in the future means that we will say "no" to things now, because we know we have better to come. To introduce this (and make your group laugh!), google "The Stanford marshmallow test", where some young children were given a marshmallow to eat, but told they could have two later on, if they didn't eat the first marshmallow in the meantime. You can watch the children attempt to resist living for the present in order to wait for a better future—it's very funny!

GUIDANCE FOR QUESTIONS

1. What motivations do people have for living in the way God wants? Possibilities include: fear, guilt, desire to go to heaven, gratitude, to repay the debt we owe him, to please him.

- **Which are good motivations, and which are not, do you think?** The aim of this question is to get your group realising that not all motivations to serve God are good ones. For instance, if we are only serving God so that we go to heaven, then really we are serving ourselves; God is just a means to an end. If we are serving God out of fear of what he'll do to us if we don't, then we will be terrified of him.

2. What has appeared, and what is significant about that (v 11)? "The grace of God." It is significant because it "offers salvation to all people". Because the grace of God appeared, salvation is on offer to everyone and anyone. (**Note:** Paul is not teaching universalism—the idea that everyone will be saved. He is clear elsewhere that not everyone will escape hell—see for instance 2 Thessalonians 1 v 6-10. Paul is teaching not that all people *will* be saved, but that what God has done means that everyone *can* be saved.) **What event do you think Paul is referring to?** The life of Jesus—his incarnation, ministry, death and resurrection. The whole sequence of events in history can be summed up as an act of grace. All of it was done with the aim of offering salvation to all people.

3. What will appear (v 13)? "The glory of our great God and Saviour, Jesus Christ." (**Note:** This probably means that God the Father's glory will be seen when Jesus Christ returns, because Jesus IS God's glory.)

4. What did the Jesus who *will* appear do when he *first* appeared (v 14)? He "gave himself for us" (in his death), to "redeem us"—pay a price to free us. Why? So that we could be purified and be his people, "eager to do what is good". The purpose of Jesus' death was not simply to free us from hell, but to make us his people, living for and like him.

5. What does Paul say Christians are waiting for (v 13)? "Blessed hope." We are waiting for Jesus to return, because that will be the start of our amazing future. It will be "blessed" (a life enjoying being the people we were designed to be). It is a "hope"—in the Bible this does not mean something that is uncertain, but something that we can be confident about.

6. APPLY: How should knowing that we live between grace and glory shape our attitude towards:
- **our mistakes?** Grace has saved us from our sins—we do not need to fear punishment for them.
- **our regrets?** Whatever we may have done, it cannot affect our ultimate future. Christ will appear in all of God's glory.
- **the parts of life we find wonderful?** There is better to come! We can be grateful for them, but we must not be complacent and think they are the best we have. The future will be even greater.
- **the parts of life we find difficult?** There is better to come! We don't need to despair.

7. APPLY: How would it affect our attitudes and lives if we forgot either that God's grace has already appeared, or that God's glory will one day appear? If grace had not appeared, we could not be saved. And we therefore would need to be terrified of God, and of death.
If glory won't appear, we have no certain hope. We won't be able to look to the future with confidence or excitement. And we will be tempted to live for the present instead.

8. What does God's grace teach us to do in life (v 12)? What do each of these phrases/words mean?
- *Say "no" to ungodliness.* Tell your group that the word "ungodliness" is often used when talking about idolatry (worshipping something more than God, as a god)—see Romans 1 v 18.
- *Be self-controlled.* This is referring to our relationship with ourselves—to have ourselves under control, rather than being under the control of our desires.
- *Be upright.* Meaning "just". In our relationship with others, grace teaches us to treat others fairly and kindly—to put them first, as God has put us first.
- *Be godly.* The opposite of "ungodliness". In our relationship with God, grace teaches us to love him, serve him and treat him as God.

9. How does God's grace and glory change:
- **our view of our future (and therefore our present) (v 13)?** We are headed for glorious perfection—we will be with Jesus, who *is* God's glory.
- **how we love (v 14a; see 1 John 4 v 19)?** Jesus "gave himself for us". And so "we love because he first loved us"

(1 John 4 v 19). Jesus gave himself for me, and his love wins my heart.

- **how we see ourselves (v 14b)?** We are God's very own people, purified to do good works.
- **How do each of these teach us to live in the way verse 12 says?**
  Future: Grace and glory show us how amazing our future with God is, and how he is better, fuller and richer than anything else—so they teach us not to worship anything else instead. We choose to live for God, instead of the immediate and visible pleasures of sin.
  Love: I serve my Saviour not to win his love, but because he has loved me so much, and I love him in return. If we know how much Jesus loves us, his grace teaches us to live in a way that loves him.
  Identity: We live in a way that matches our identity. We know we are Christ's, so we want to live like Christ. We become "eager to do what is good" because of who we are.

10. What is Titus to do with this truth (v 15)? He is to teach this—both in encouraging people, but also in rebuking people. Past grace and the future glory are to be the content of his teaching. **What should we want our own church leaders to do with this?** To teach it to us! We need to resist the urge to want leaders to teach something "new" or "advanced" instead of the gospel of what God has done and what God will do. And we need to be prepared and willing to be challenged by our church leaders, when we need it.

EXPLORE MORE
Read Hebrews 11 v 24-26. How is Moses a great example of the way in which grace teaches us to live in our present?

He knew that a "reward" lay ahead of him; so he lived as part of God's people, instead of enjoying "the fleeting pleasures of sin". Notice his perspective—sinning was only a "fleeting pleasure". He shows us not to live for what we can have now, but for what we know we will have in the future.
What would it mean for you to live like Moses in your culture and context?

11. APPLY: What motivations does this passage give us for living the way God wants? Refer back to Q9. The chief motives are where we are headed (glory, being with Christ); how we love (supremely God, who loves us so much); and who we are (Christ's people, for whom he died to purify and make his own).

12. APPLY: Take a couple of areas where all or several of you find Christian obedience hard. How does this passage shape your thinking about those areas? For each, think about how your future, your love and your identity shapes your thinking in that area. Be specific.

5 Titus 3 v 1-15
STRESS THESE THINGS

THE BIG IDEA
We need to stress the kindness and love of God in saving us through the work of his Son and his Spirit; and avoid getting sidetracked by arguments or controversies.

SUMMARY
Paul is focusing here on the time in the past when God's grace appeared. Now, he describes it as "the kindness and love of God our Saviour" appearing (v 4).

But that description of God's kindness is prefaced with a hard truth about us in verse 3—our relationship with God was a mess, and our relationships with each other were therefore also a mess. We will never understand the wonderful kindness of God until we face the reality of what we are like without him.

Verse 3 shows us just how kind God is, to save (v 5) people like us. He saves us not because of anything in us, but because of his mercy. Then in v 4-7, Paul explains how God saved us. First, it was through the appearing of his Son, our Saviour (v 4), to justify us (v 7). The verdict on us should be "guilty"—but God's Son took the sentence we deserve, dying in our place to pay our penalty. Then, God's Spirit "rebirth[ed]" us (v 5). He opens our eyes to recognise Jesus as our Saviour, so we put our faith in him.

Having described the gospel in this "trustworthy saying" (v 8: verses 3-7 may be an early hymn, or creed), Paul then tells Titus to "stress these things" (v 8). We can never talk about the gospel too much. What we and our church family most need is to have these things stressed, again and again. This is "profitable for everyone" (v 8).

This means we need to "avoid foolish controversies" (v 9), which are "unprofitable and useless". It is easy to put our energy into arguments and quarrels—Paul urges Titus (and us) to put it into stressing the gospel. We see Paul modelling this in his attitude towards Apollos (v 13—see Explore More).

As we "stress" the gospel as a church, we learn to "devote [ourselves] to doing what is good"—living the "good life" which is the purpose of Paul's letter to Titus (v 8). Verses 1-2 give part of the shape of that life: submission to authorities, and gentleness to those around us (even when they respond in the malice and envy that characterise our natural state, v 3). Paul repeats his desire for Christians to be devoted to living this "good" life in verse 14: as we reflect on and enjoy the gospel of verses 3-7, we'll live the gospel life, the good life, the missional life.

OPTIONAL EXTRA
Verses 3-7 are one long sentence in the original Greek. So challenge your group, in turn, to speak the longest sentence they can, without pause, hesitation or repetition. You could also challenge them to read verses 3-7 as one sentence, ignoring the full stops/periods, without taking a breath.

GUIDANCE FOR QUESTIONS
1. How do you think of God? What words do you use to describe him? Ask people to limit their responses to single words or short sentences!

2. What uncomfortable truths about ourselves do we discover in verse 3? We were:

- foolish—in the Bible, a fool is someone who acts as though there is no God eg: Psalm 14 v 1.
- disobedient—whether or not we acknowledged God, we did not obey him.

This rejection of God affected our thinking (we were deceived) and we could not sort it out—we were enslaved by our foolish disobedience. We were trapped by our sinful habits.

Because our relationship with God was in a mess, our relationships with each other were, too: "We lived in malice and envy, being hated and hating one another".

⊻

- **Do you recognise this is what you were/are naturally like? How does it make you feel?** The reality is that we will never understand what God has done for us in verse 4 until we face the reality of what we are like without him.

3. How is this appearing described here (v 4-5a)?

- As the coming of "the kindness and love of God our Saviour" (v 4). Point out that these are the two words Paul uses to describe the God who came as Jesus— kind and loving.
- "He saved us" (v 5a). This, of course, is referring to Christ's death in our place, taking the punishment that our foolish disobedience towards God and our malice and envy towards each other deserve.

4. Why did God save us (v 5)? Not
because of anything we have done ("righteous things"). Only "because of his mercy". God did not think we were, on balance, OK; or that we had potential. He knew we were the people of verse 3—and he had mercy on us because he loves us.

5. What is the Holy Spirit's role in saving us? Verse 5—the "washing of rebirth and renewal". "Rebirth" captures the idea that we are dead, and then born. The Holy Spirit brings us to life by opening our eyes to see who Jesus is and to put our faith in him. In his kindness and love, God the Father saves us through his Son, and gives us faith in his Son through the work of his Spirit. We are totally renewed.

Note: "The washing" is probably a reference to baptism—but this does not mean that baptism is the moment at which rebirth takes place (that happens when the Spirit gives us faith in Jesus). Baptism is the outward sign of the inward reality—the great celebration and sign of God's initiative in regeneration.

6. How do these verses help us to "measure" the kindness and love of God?

Try to measure it in terms of...

- *what God has given.* He has given us himself. He has kindly and lovingly given us his Son (v 4). And he has generously poured out on us his Spirit (v 6). There is nothing more God could have given.
- *what God has done.* He has done everything. He has justified us, with no cost to us and at great cost to himself (v 7). He has given us new birth; he has renewed us (v 5). Every step of the way, he has provided. Everything that was needed and is needed he has done and is doing. There is nothing more that he could have done.
- *what God has promised.* He has promised us eternal life in a world reborn (v 7, see 1 v 2-3). He saved us to become heirs, looking forward with certain hope to an eternity spent enjoying all that Christ deserves (v 7). This is "the hope of eternal life", and it is promised by God, "who

does not lie" (1 v 2). There is nothing more that he could have promised.

7. APPLY: Share with your group which truth about God's kindness particularly thrills you today. It might be helpful to give your group a minute in quiet to think about and (if they want to) write down their answer, before you share responses. You might like to have a time of thanksgiving, to turn the responses into prayers of praise.

8. How do verses 3-5 prevent us feeling:
- **proud?** Verse 3 shows us that all we bring to our salvation is our sin. We have contributed nothing to the rescue. Nothing we are or do in the Christian life deserves our relationship with God or our future with him.
- **worthless or hopeless?** Despite the truth about who we are, God in his kindness loves us so much that he sent his Son to die for us, and his Spirit to give us new life by giving us faith in Jesus' death. We have great worth in God's eyes. And we have a wonderful future—however difficult or desolate life is right now, the Spirit has been poured into us, and glory lies ahead of us. There is always hope.

9. What should Titus:
- **remind his church about (v 1-2)?**
  - To be subject to authority—and not only this, but proactively to "be ready to do whatever is good". We should be looking for opportunities to bless our cities and serve our neighbours.
  - To avoid slandering, and to be peaceful (literally, "don't quarrel"), considerate and gentle. Notice how different this is to who we naturally are (v 3)—and how the world often treats us. The challenge is to be gentle in the face of malice and envy.

- **stress to his church (v 8)?** "These things"—that is, the kindness and love of God in saving people like us.
- **avoid (v 9)?** Controversies, arguments, and quarrels—things that are unprofitable and useless (unlike stressing the gospel, which is profitable, v 8). These are "divisive" (v 10).

10. Why do you think Paul uses such strong language in verses 10-11 (think about the letter as a whole)? Christ "gave himself for us" to make "a people" (2 v 14)—a united church. Acting in a way that is divisive goes against God's eternal plan. So when someone sows disunity among gospel believers, the purposes of God, the work of the cross and the sake of mission are all at stake. That's why Paul tells Titus to warn, then warn again, and finally to put out of the church ("have nothing to do with") someone who continues to divide God's people.

EXPLORE MORE
What does Paul want Titus to do for Apollos and Zenas (v 13)? Everything he can to help them, giving them everything they need.
Read 1 Corinthians 1 v 11-12. Why might Paul have been tempted to hinder, or at best not to help, Apollos in his ministry? What is impressive about Titus 3 v 13? Apollos was being touted as Paul's "rival", with many in the Corinthian church (which Paul had founded) loudly preferring Apollos and shunning Paul. So it would be easy for Paul to feel competitive, or bitter, towards Apollos. At least, it would be easy for Paul to tolerate Apollos' ministry, but not to help it. Yet here in Titus 3 v 13, he wants Titus to do everything possible to help Apollos and his ministry.

Read 1 Corinthians 3 v 1-9. What truths about ministry meant that Paul wanted to support Apollos, not compete with him? Neither Paul nor Apollos are the ones who grow gospel ministry—that is God. And neither Paul nor Apollos deserve the praise—that is God, too. So there is no need for (or room for) ministry competition—Paul wants Apollos to have everything he needs to continue to preach and "stress" the gospel, for the glory of God.

11. APPLY: Why do we often find ourselves focusing on disagreements and quarrels, rather than the gospel? Because we are still, naturally, the people of Titus 3 v 3. So malice and envy are never far from our hearts. Our sin and pride and self-righteousness come out in us devoting our time and words and energies to stressing controversy instead of the gospel. Dispute seems more interesting and exciting to us than the "same old" gospel truths.

12. APPLY: How, practically, can we "stress these things"—that is, the content of verses 3-8a—in our conversations and lives? Encourage your group to think of specific, real, regular situations. And encourage them to think about how exactly they would stress what God has done, and what that means, in those situations.

What's your question?

Who on earth is the Holy Spirit?
And other questions about who He is and what He does
Tim Chester and Christopher de la Hoyde

Is forgiveness really free?
And other questions about grace, the law and being saved
Michael Jensen

Why did Jesus have to die?
And other questions about the cross of Christ and its meaning for us today
Marcus Nodder

Everyone has questions. The **Questions Christians Ask** series offers answers in a short, accessible way. Each book gives applied, relevant and personal teaching on a crucial subject.

What happens when I die?
And other questions about heaven, hell and the life to come
Marcus Nodder

Is God anti-gay?
And other questions about homosexuality, the Bible and same-sex attraction
Sam Allberry

Did the devil make me do it?
And other questions about Satan, demons and evil spirits
Mike McKinley

Find out more at:
www.thegoodbook.com/qca

Dig deeper into Titus

TITUS
FOR YOU

In this, the fourth in a brand-new ground-breaking series, Tim brings his trademark clarity, grace and insight to the book of Titus. Written for Christians of every age and stage, whether new believers or pastors and teachers, each title in the series takes a detailed look at a part of the Bible in a readable, relevant way.

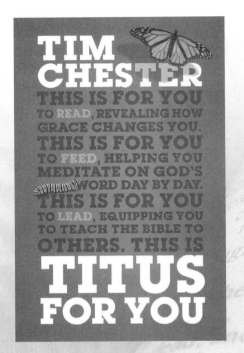

Titus For You is for you:

- *to read,* mapping out the themes and challenges of the epistle.
- *to feed,* using it as a daily devotional, complete with helpful reflection questions.
- *to lead,* equipping small-group leaders and Bible teachers and preachers to explain, illustrate and apply this wonderful book of the Bible.

Find out more at:
www.thegoodbook.com/for-you

with Tim Chester

EXPLORE DAILY BIBLE STUDIES

These notes will help encourage and equip you each day for your walk with God. Available as a book or as an app, *Explore* features notes on Titus, as well as Tim's studies on Ruth, 2 Samuel, Isaiah and Hosea. Other contributors include Tim Keller, Christopher Ash, Mark Dever, Graham Beynon, Ray Ortlund and John Hindley.

Find out more at:
www.thegoodbook.com/explore

Good Book Guides
for groups and individuals

Elijah: A Man Just Like Us

Liam Goligher
Senior Minister of Tenth Presbyterian Church,
Philadelphia

Elijah was a man just like us—not so much
a mighty man as a man who served the
mighty God. Elijah's ups and downs speak
to us too.

Ezekiel: The God of Glory

Tim Chester
Pastor of The Crowded House, Sheffield, UK

"Then they will know that I am the LORD"
is the repeated message of Ezekiel. In a
world of false hopes that will ultimately
fail, this is a message for everyone.

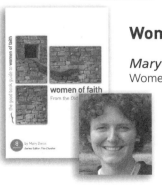

Women of Faith

Mary Davis
Women's Ministry Director, St Nicholas Church,
Tooting, UK

Examine the lives and experiences of seven
women from the Old Testament; their flaws,
faith, struggles and solutions.

To see all 38 titles in the range, visit:
www.thegoodbook.com/goodbookguides

1 Corinthians: Challenging Church

Mark Dever
Senior Pastor of Capitol Hill Baptist Church in Washington
DC and President of 9Marks Ministries

The church in Corinth was full of life, and full of
problems. As you read how Paul challenges these
Christians, you'll see how you can help shape your
own church to become truly gospel-centred.

Ephesians: God's Big Plan for Christ's New People

Thabiti Anyabwile
Senior Pastor, First Baptist Church, Grand Cayman,
USA

If we would be healthy Christians, we would
be wise to build our lives around the kind
of church that emerges from the book of
Ephesians.

Romans 1-7: The Gift of God

Timothy Keller
Senior Pastor, Redeemer Presbyterian Church, Manhattan

Romans is about right standing with God—why
we don't have it, why we need it, how we can
receive it—and how it transforms our hearts, lives,
identities and perspectives.

thegoodbook
COMPANY

thegoodbook
COMPANY

Opening up the Bible

At The Good Book Company, we are dedicated to helping Christians and local churches grow. We believe that God's growth process always starts with hearing clearly what he has said to us through his timeless word—the Bible.

Ever since we opened our doors in 1991, we have been striving to produce resources that honor God in the way the Bible is used. We have grown to become an international provider of user-friendly resources to the Christian community, with believers of all backgrounds and denominations using our Bible studies, books, evangelistic resources, DVD-based courses and training events.

We want to equip ordinary Christians to live for Christ day by day, and churches to grow in their knowledge of God, their love for one another, and the effectiveness of their outreach.

Call us for a discussion of your needs or visit one of our local websites for more information on the resources and services we provide.

North America: www.thegoodbook.com
UK & Europe: www.thegoodbook.co.uk
Australia: www.thegoodbook.com.au
New Zealand: www.thegoodbook.co.nz

North America: 866 244 2165
UK & Europe: 0333 123 0880
Australia: (02) 6100 4211
New Zealand (+64) 3 343 1990

www.christianityexplored.org

Our partner site is a great place for those exploring the Christian faith, with a clear explanation of the good news, powerful testimonies and answers to difficult questions.

One life. What's it all about?